Micro-Novels

73/100

Tony Sellen

Micro-Novels

Tory Seller

Tory Seller Publications
Los Angeles, California U.S.A.

Printed in the United States of America

First Printing, 2018

Cover design by Brice Frillici

ISBN 978-0-692-12960-9

Address all inquiries to:

TORY SELLER PUBLICATIONS

200 Valley Dr. Suite 56
Brisbane, CA 94005

email: torysellerpublications@gmail.com

www.facebook.com/MicroNovelsTorySeller

DEDICATED

To
Stephanie Jo Foradas
&
Mikel Ross,

for believing in me.

Acknowledgements

This book would not be possible without my Facebook friends, many of whom I've had the pleasure of meeting in person. For keeping me in line and inspiring me, in no particular order: Charlie Smackus, Brice Frillici, Freddie Claudio, Jeff Johnson, Jonathan Framstad, Robert Hope, Sunna Ward, Jamie Augustine, Laurel Bayleaf, Travis Kasperbauer, Bieneke Bien, Charlie Sixer, George Vigil, Iain Sorrie, Matthew Kaney, Mimi Tolva, John DiScala, Ms. G. and many, many more, thank you.

Table of Contents

"An Introduction to the Micro-Novel" by Jeff Johnson

What is a *Micro-Novel*, you ask? A poem? Another exercise in avante garde dipshittery?

nov·el1

ˈnävəl/

noun

a fictitious prose narrative of book length, typically representing character and action with some degree of realism.

So a micro-novel would be what?? Let's turn to another word before we begin the exploration.

ko·an

ˈkōän/

noun

a paradoxical anecdote or riddle, used in Zen Buddhism to demonstrate the inadequacy of logical reasoning and to provoke enlightenment.

Bob Seger, Zen Buddhism, The Easter Bunny, well, we're still lost. Let's take a look at the mind behind the micro novel. Without further adieu, let's descend into an introduction to the enigmatic Tory Seller himself.

I met Tory in San Francisco a few years ago. I'd been invited down for an all expenses paid writing gig. A script was coming together for HBO about a hippy commune, and while it wasn't exactly my genre, it was close enough. Tory was one of the other writers, a bearded, quiet, very stoned guy, but friendly enough. We got to work.

By day two it became apparent that this was not, in fact, an all expense paid gig, nor was it going to HBO. Unfortunately, this coincided with other bad news. My agent at the time was an absolute cretin. He lost my new novel, and I had to use Tory's computer to rescue a copy from my sent email. I then had to use his computer to finish it a second time. The novel was *Deadbomb Bingo Ray*. I did this in Tory's car as we rolled around late night San Francisco, working night after night in the halo of weed he surrounded himself with. He waxed on and on about the local hookers, parakeets, experimental music, Australia, glue, what have you, and we became friends. My then agent went on to misplace the publisher's contract, so I was stranded for another week. It was then, while we were living off Tory's food stamps and sleeping on couches in the lobby of a recording studio, that I was first introduced to the micro novel.

Each segment was crafted, and not in a pedantic, fussy way. Tory was not operating in the quiet of his home at night after he'd worked all day in a bookstore or an office. This was not engineered in a cafe workshop or his mother's basement either. He was in motion, a strange hybrid of outlaw and surfer, with a generous helping of The Dude in his character profile. The snips, the condensed microsities, had been streamlined in a Beat fashion, shorn of verbiage, adjectives, dead weight, live action, conjecture, structure, all of it. They were encapsulations distilled by momentum, sculpted by roads, delivered through spiritual digestion.

Another week passed while my agent fumbled the money for the novel. I was stranded for one more week before I finally bypassed him. In that week, I watched Tory create, and I'm glad I did. It was an amazingly involved process, and unique in my experience. A novelist sits. Thinks. Writes for hours. Repeats. A micro novelist does something very different.

Creating the micro-novel, any of them, involved driving. Tory talks to himself, even when you're in the car with him. He stops and stares at things. He writes on napkins. He takes notes on his phone. The micro novel is alive because of it.

Read these in the car. Read them on the toilet. Read them on a train. Mutter the words under your breath as you do, and consider them from various angles. Memorize your favorites and repeat them to people at awkward times. Leave your copy at the airport when you're done, or give it to your boss for Christmas. Because that's what this is. It's a gift from a stranger to a stranger. Quickly now! Turn to the next page and-

Jeff Johnson
Portland, Oregon 2018

Micro-Novels

"Monday"

Monday is a great day to take chances.

"Goals"

Goals for today:

1.) Leave the house.

2.) Take a shower.

I did the kitty litter get off my back.

"Target Parking Lot"

I saw her in the parking lot. White Mercedes, high maintenance, I was doin' batties listening to Olav Basoski*. She looked at me, I looked at her. She was on the phone, I was in my car. Target parking lot.

* Olav Basoski - Very Disco (1999)

"The Lonely Janitor"

Writing's a lonely job. But it's better than being a janitor.

"Bruce Willis"

Chick just waved at me with a bunny rabbit glove on.
That's the way most Bruce Willis movies start.

"Get Up"

Got up, the stash sip of coffee saved my ass, smashed the mirror off my car last night, wasn't lookin' forward to the light. The sun shone, feng shui stellar, mild morning, Asians walk by my car. Get up.

"Escargot"

I just ordered escargot stuffed off the menu at the local Vietnamese place. I wouldn't have done that on Monday.

"Undercover Boss"

I walked into the office for my third cup of coffee,
new kid training, seven-hour early check-in I like this
place. I walked toward the front desk, lifted up my
sunglasses. "I just wanted to let you know, I'm Steve
Jenkins, CEO of 'Motel 6'; you're on 'Undercover
Boss'". Pause. Reaction. I'm so fuckin' awesome.
P.S. Later.

"Adequate (I Try to Write Part 3)"

I have one to three ideas in my head, I stumble around the coffee table. The computer screen blinds me, I jot down one to three ideas.

I take a leak.

I pet my cat.

"Adequate: A Cologne Bi Tory Seller".

"Fish Tacos"

I hit a big deadline,
I made fish tacos.

"Ghetto Wing"

Ghetto is: Heating up the oven for one gluten-free chicken wing.

"Stay Hungry"

Ya kinda gotta get hungry to get hungry do ya know what I mean?

"Wendy's"

I just got two orders of free fries from "Wendy's".
Old bag wanted "hot fries". I said "Are you gonna
throw those away?" I also said "Kids starvin' in India"
to cover how broke I am. She wants me.

P.S. This story is more depressing to me than it is to
you.

P.P.S. Later.

"Chemtrails Part 3"

Chemtrails dissipate.

"Science"

Science now says that masturbation and marijuana are good for you. I may live to be four hundred years old.

"A Trap(International Pirate Day/Enjoying Paranoia Part 12)"

The girl at McDonald's said she liked my shirt, "It's 'International Pirate Day'". She said she liked my "cologne" also. She was young, it felt like a trap.

"Alfred E. Neuman"

I looked in the mirror this morning and saw Alfred E. Newman. The end.

"California"

I gave her my card, I told her I could make her a star.
She said she already had an agent.

"Val Kilmer(That is All Part 96)"

My driver's license came in the mail today, I look like Val Kilmer in "Heat". That is all.

"2025(No Pressure)"

I keep telling myself I'm going to have kids. I keep pushing it back five years. Every five years. I think I'm doing it to keep my Mom alive. Maybe it's vanity. With that said, I am looking for an individual to squeeze me out a puppy by 2025. No pressure.

"Deep Thoughts 69.23"

I'm thinkin' about leaving the house today.

"Agoraphobic Dream Come True"

The only time I really leave the house is to deposit money when a check bounces.

"The Longest Yard"

The guy at the dispensary said I looked like "Burt Reynolds in 'Boogie Nights'". I feel like I'm in "The Longest Yard".

"Hello(Andrea's Gone)"

The blind chick Andrea's gone, she moved out of the building. I used to have these fantasies about seducing her, like Lionel Richie in the music video "Hello". "Hello, is it me you're lookin' for?" I guess not. Your lose, talk to the hand.

"Writer Observations Part 5"

If you write fifteen hours a day there will be improvements.

"Distinctive Mustache(Burning Man 2009)"

I'm about 89% sure I found the guy I hung out with at "Burning Man 2009". He had a distinctive mustache.

"Chemtrails(How I Learned to Love Chemtrails and Myself Part 1)"

Pretty chemtrails.
Chemtrails pretty.

"Coke"

I hate coke. The end.

"Extra Sprinkles(Success)"

Sprinkles
over

icing.

Success.

"Tory Seller: Hair Model"

Just got a gig as a hair model. I use good
conditioner.

"Lesbians(Deep Thoughts 439)"

Been thinkin' for hours……..Haven't eaten' much……..Why do lesbians have to be so hot……..The end.

"Note to Self Part 1(Bang Hookers)"

Note to self:
Don't buy a whole pie, you don't have a
family...........
(Insert "Full House" Meme)
Score coke.
Bang hookers.
Later.

P.S. I hate coke, it just rhymed better with smoke.

P.P.S. Later.

"Roofies'"

callin mom and goin to bed i took the roofies

"Dear Online Mistress"

Dear Online Mistress,

I just pinched my nipple for 12 seconds as instructed. Thank you Mistress.

"Cat Move"

Cat doesn't move for an hour
comes back and takes a leak
with me.

"The Problem with Cocaine(Johnny B. Goode)"

The problem with cocaine: "Johnny B. Goode" by Judas Priest. The end.

"The String Cheese Incident"

I like to give TNC vehicle rides between 4:15 and 5:30 in the morning, on the weekends. People are either trippin'' balls, or tweakin', I adjust my conversations accordingly. I picked up a guy from the "String Cheese Incident" concert, and you know you know, so I dropped a subtle mushroom hint twelve seconds into his ride. This silly guy dropped an eighth in my car, and I didn't know whether to call the police or flush 'em down the toilet. I flushed 'em down the toilet.

"My Ex"

My ex said she's "proud of me". Me too, I didn't kill her.

"Overdraft Problems(Bondage Gear)"

I bought too much bondage gear last night and got an overdraft fee. The end..

"Duct Tape"

I Like Duct Tape. The end.

"The Johnny Carson Show(We'll Be Right Back)"

JOHNNY CARSON: Well Tory, you're lookin' good, how ya feelin'….

TORY SELLER: Not bad Johnny, my girlfriend fingered my ass last night. I tried to talk her into three fingers, but she said she didn't wanna hurt me.......She's so sweet..."

JOHNNY CARSON: Well........then........We'll be right back……"

"Replacement Muse(Kicked Out of Mensa)"

I told baby to hang in there three years and I'll buy her that Pink Lamborghini I've been wantin' to get her. After that, she can pick up bad boys while I work on a "Replacement Muse", nineteen, kicked out of Mensa.

"Nosey Ass"

I might be
manic nosey ass.

"Fourth Floor"

The lady across the street is trying out her new camera, snappin' pictures and such. I pulled up my shirt and twisted my nipple she lives on the fourth floor.

"A Better Person(Lies We Tell Ourselves)"

I'm brushing my teeth
longer I'm going to be
a better person.

"Social Anxiety or Hatred of People Part 2"

On the rare occasions I leave the house I usually piss people off. That's why I try not to leave the house.

"Interesting Fact #22"

I brush my teeth in my sweater sometimes in my car.

"Spring Fever"

I was lookin' right at her. Right at her pussy, I was on
an incline headin' east as the sun set bitch don't
wear spandex if you don't want me lookin' you like
it.

"Bad Girls"

i like bad girls

"Dirty"

I'm so fuckin' dirty showers help.

"Men Are Terrible(Me Too)"

Men are terrible, me too. What can you do?

"How to Pick Up Chicks on Fakebook"

How to Pick Up Chicks on Fakebook:

Rule One: Don't even think about sendin' a "DM" until the second month.

Rule Two: See rule one.

"Baby Carriage(Dolores Park)"

I noticed the MILF when I parked the car.
Baby carriage.
You don't get MILFIER than that.
Designer sunglasses,
cocker-spaniel fetching a ball.
Up and down.
Up and down.

Dolores Park.

"Facebook Politics"

I just deleted my Mom.

"WOOF"

I barked pretty loudly today,
I felt it in my diaphragm.
I'm a dog.
dog WOOF.

"Facebook Advertisements"

Facebook just paid me $700,000.

"Becoming a Writer"

Now I really feel like a writer, I just had my cable turned off, voluntarily, don't get cheeky.

"Suffice"

Five different kinds of weed suffice to say I'll be writing all day. Suffice.

"Amber Alerts"

My feelings on Amber alerts: I don't have any kids. I don't know an Ambers. If I see Amber, I will tell her to give you a call. Thank you for your time and consideration.

"3 A.M."

"No new friends after 3 A.M.", it's a simple rule I made in Seattle walkin' the streets on a graveyard listenin' to Frankie Knuckle's "Live in Argentina"(I love that mix). No lighter, no cigarettes, I'm not your friend after three in the morning. 3 A.M.

"I Am Timothy Leary"

My neighbor looks like Timothy Leary, fifty-five I'm guessin', fifty-three, Leary at his peak or just past. We smoke scoob and chat, we mind our own business. I watch the brahs play golf across the street, I pet cats. I play techno music. I am Timothy Leary.

"Cannabis"

So you live in Europe. You don't do drugs anymore. You're going out with friends tonight. You still like house music. Cannabis is not a drug.

"Go Figure"

The cool thing about not owning much stuff is it's easy to find your stuff. The bad part is you don't own much stuff go figure.

"Ultra Violence(Go Figure Part Two)"

I'm smoking "Ultra Violence" and I'm feelin' "kinda mellow" go figure.

"Burning Man"

If "Burning Man" is walking around the apartment naked with a banana in your hand I'm already there, I'm at Burning Man.

"Breakfast"

Some people say breakfast is the most important meal of the day. I hate those people.

"Priorities"

I bought ninety-one dollars worth of books today. I
slept in my car.
Priorities.

"Monarch Butterflies(I Know Lesbians)"

I have a hook-up on "Monarch Butterflies", that's not code for anything, I know lesbians.

"Colorado"

If you
wanna take a drive
Get deep
Be lovers
for the week
Let me know.

Colorado.

"Pierre"

I'm in my underwear, door open, my neighbor stops
by, social services shrink but doesn't understand
personal space, retired. We talk about the cat and
I'm in my underwear and we're pretty close and she
tells me about her boyfriend in Belgium and how
she's going to live with him in a month like I give a
fuck I know the story lady you've told me a hundred
fucking times it's eight in the morning. His name is
"Pierre".

"Fuck You(Chevy Aveo)"

Writin' at stoplights bitch thought he was going to pass me on the Eight, not today, it was completely unnecessary to take it up to eighty-two on a Monday afternoon but I did it anyway, actin' all hard in your Chevy Aveo or whatever the fuck it is, I heard Bukowski in the backseat "pass that motherfucker." I lined up even and looked over, he knowed he was beat actin' all hard in your Chevy Aveo at eleven-thirty on a Monday afternoon or whatever the fuck it is, fuck you.

"Pistachios"

She was abrasive at first but she gave me her number, wants me to help her with her "social networking". She had beers in her gym bag who am I to judge? Says she's going to the casino, hasn't had a date in a year. A disabled guy offered to buy her a sandwich, she gave me pistachios.

"Minnesota"

I saw a Minnesota license plate yesterday and thought of you.

(Insert Don Henley Song)

"The Lie(4006 Friends)"

I lied because it was easier
I hate betrayal the most
Eliminated hope
And now I delete you
off my Facebook page

I wish I felt better
but I don't

I'll feel better when
you're dead though that's

just the

truth

I'm sure you won't take
it personally

4006 Friends.

"Facebook is a Dating Site"

Remember when Facebook was fun? When you deleted your whole family because they inhibited your writing? Boy, I sure do. Anyway, I'm here to remind you: Facebook is fun! Political post, charitable cause, not on my watch. BDSM, swingers club, now we're talkin', remember, Facebook is a dating site. Thank you.

"9 A.M."

I've been writing since 9 A.M., these are the days I'll remember.

"Anger Control Problems"

One of the great things about having anger control problems is the people in your building tend to leave you alone.

"The Girlfriend Experience"

I like to hire hookers to complain and watch "Netflix" with me. I call it "The Girlfriend Experience".

"Sprouts Parking Lot"

Real men eat kimchi. If anybody wants to fight about it, meet me in the "Sprouts" parking lot after three I have yoga thanks.

"Direction"

When I'm feeling down, or questioning my direction in life, I look at my bank account and buy as much weed as I can. And then I smoke it.

P.S. The end.

"Duets"

I like duets. Tired of singing both parts.

"The Jerk"

I like to flirt with the old ladies in my building. Probably because I hardly ever leave the building. I saw the old lady with the cane, probably about fifty-two fumblin' her keys in front of the building. "Hey, you know that movie 'The Jerk' right, 'The new phonebooks are here, the new phone books are here!' I thought I was the only one that would understand that." "No I understood it." I'm so gonna bone her later.

"What Women Really Want Part 73"

What Women Really Want Part 73:

Humor,
and
indifference.

(Fuck off)

"How I Deal with Bi-Polar 2(Make a Decision)"

Make a decision. Make that decision every day. Try to make it in the morning. Make a decision. If you're manic, breath, slow down a little, jerk off, write, bring it in a little. If you're depressed, get up, do some push-ups, take a walk, jerk off, throw on some porn, that's how I deal with bi-polar 2: Make a decision.

"Micro-Dosing"

On micro-dosing: One man's micro-dose is another man's macro-dose, and vice versa, do you.

"I Play Piano"

Joined a country band last week, God I'm bad. I play piano.

"Competition"

I wanna be the writer that
makes you change

majors or instruments

I'm competitive.

"Pistachios Part 2"

Long term goals
I want to grow pistachios.

"Trimmin' Bud(I Like Baby Buds)"

Trimmin' Bud

God I hate it some people like big buds I like baby buds when you're at the bottom of the barrel and you see a baby bud glistens in the sunlight I like baby buds.

"Chest"

November 19, 2017 5:08 P.M.

Dabbed. I haven't had a dab in awhile, not since San Francisco at least, I'm high as fuck and I'm sitting in the "Planet Fitness" parking lot. I'll work-out, shower, get on the massage table and leave. I'm homeless. Not like skid row homeless, more like I have social anxiety and I'd rather be broke than deal with dumb fucks. My buddy's meeting with Sean Penn's manager today, it puts a smile on my face. I'm thinkin' about goin' to see a girl I met on Facebook, what's new? She's pretty awesome, and her tits are so big her back hurts all the time. We've been talkin' on the phone off and on for about a year. She's crazy, but I trust her. And the tits. Anyway, I'm going into work-out now: Chest.

"A Great Life"

I have a better life than anyone I know I slept in my
car last night.

"Tribal(Buglachema)"

Three time ayahuasca champ

"Buglachema" stirs the potion

in a Upper middle-class neighborhood

North of Marin

You know the deal

Baby's crying

"It's natural"

Bone through the nose

Watchin' Youtube

Where does it stop

Tribal

"I Like Hookers"

I care......

Just kiddin'.......

I hate myself.
I like hookers.

The end.

"History Lessons"

I just had an old friend remind me that my longest
relationship is six months, not ten weeks.
Everybody's a historian.

"I Love Stephy Jo"

I Love Stephy Jo. The end.

"A Mistake (I Play Piano Part 2)"

I left the house today without playing piano. I won't make that mistake again.

"Work Ethics"

One thing I've learned over the years is that it's not too hard to get a job. It's not that hard to quit one either.

"Deep Conversations"

I'm dating again. I like ass-play and deep conversations. Ass-play, and then deep conversations.

"Forty-Five Minutes"

What happens when you take "Adderall" and "Cialis" at the same time? I'm not sure, but I'll tell you in forty-five minutes.

"Soft Revenge"

I have an old hard-boiled egg in the fridge. I call it "Soft Revenge".

"Advice for my Future Son"

I'm goin' to the strip club, good deals on Monday dayshift. Only two songs I get a lap-dance to: "Stranglehold" and "Stairway to Heaven".

"I Like Branding(Accommodating Skin)"

I'm not really into marriage, not at all, my Mom was married four times, anyway, if I'm gonna make a commitment like that I say branding, go branding, warm metal on accommodating skin, branding, I like branding. The end.

"Blind People"

Seattle has the highest population of blind people in America. I have a blind lady in my building, "Hey Andrea, what's up?" "Who's that?" I've introduced myself a couple times, and I don't wear much deodorant. People are so inconsiderate.

"Anita Baker"

Just another rainy day singin' "Anita Baker" songs to my cat who wants to fight?

"Little Games"

They like the Pho' up here in the Pacific Northwest,
my cats think they're gonna get some. "No Pho' Pho'
You" I say, we play little games like that.

"Social Media"

So let's see, I have a "Twitter" account, a "Facebook" account, a "Vine", "Tumblr", "Instagram", "Reddit", and "Google +". What was I saying again?

"Long Distance Relationships"

I like long distance relationships, the further away the better.

"Ink Master(Grateful Part 3)"

"Ink Master" marathon.

Lube.

A mirror on the
hotel ceiling.

Things I'm Grateful for
Part 3.

"Frank Zappa"

Frank Zappa was a great American. Frank Zappa was not from St. Louis.

"Safewords"

Light bondage scene next time I'll pick a better safe word.

"Social Anxiety or Hatred of People"

Social anxiety or hatred of people: I'm fine, I just hate people.

"Karate and Tap-Dancing "

I think I'm gonna take up tap-dancing and karate, not at the same time.

"Smucker's Jar"

You're runnin' low on weed, you're not quite at crisis mode, but you still might punch a motherfucker in the head. You can get to the dispensary in eighteen minutes, it's rainin', it could get sketchy. Surprise stash in the Smucker's jar.

"Irvine Welsh"

Irvine Welsh wrote "Trainspotting" while riding the bus around America. He was ridin' the bus.

"Coca-Cola"

(Insert mountain-climbing .jpeg)

Drink a Coke.

"Bubble Hash"

bu
bbl
e hash
by the
be
ach
it could
be worse

"Seattle Paradox"

Seattle Paradox: Construction worker blastin' opera.

"Karate Moves(Gulf War Vet)"

I'm doin' karate moves outside my hotel room just so people think I'm a Gulf War Vet. I'm a Gulf War Vet.

P.S. I'm not a Gulf War Vet.

"Seattle(That is All Part 43)"

The girls dress so swell in Seattle. That is all.

"Aikido(Just So You Know Part 24)"

Gonna start takin' aikido just so you should know.

"Cracker Barrel(Limp)"

Limp.

People limp

in and out of

Cracker Barrel.

I don't eat there much.

I don't wanna limp.

Limp, lump, limp.

The end.

"Rock Talkin'"

I was talkin' to my crystal rock I got down in San Diego when I had too much money and we were dancin' around the apartment to "Re-light My Fire" by Dan Hartman and I looked at my rock and said "Thanks for being my rock."

"Bi-Polar 2"

I like bi-polar 2 'cause the cycles are shorter and not as intense that's why I like bi-polar 2 the end.

"Ambien"

A TNC customer dropped an "Ambien" in my car. I just flushed it down the toilet.

"Regret"

dood regretting neck tattoo

"How to Negotiate(A Compliment Part 2)"

You're biggest strength is patience. It's a busy world. People wanna shake your hand and get ya out the door. Sit down. Pour some coffee. Walk slow. Talk slow. Be slow. Slow. Slow. Slow.

"White Privilege Part Somethin'"

White Privilege + Anarchy = Good Time.

"Condensed(The Life of Jim Morrison)"

the life of Jim Morrison condensed
keep your eyes on the road the end

"Condensed(The Life of Jim Morrison Part 2)"

break on through the end

"Condensed(The Life of Jim Morrison Part 3)"

the end

"Ambien Part 2"

"Ambien" "ShmAmbien" I need a lift.

"I Like Seattle"

I like Seattle 'cause you can see your blind neighbor walkin' across the street with a six pack talkin' on the phone. I like Seattle.

"Compliments"

The best compliment is no compliment at all.

"Grammar"

From my brief experience on the "Facebook", I think people from the Midwest have incredible grammatical abilities. I'm from the Midwest.

"Mayweather vs. McGregor"

I watched the Mayweather* fight with some lesbians, they were nice, they fed me. I kept quiet when Jen stood up and said "I'm going to get a wiener, does anybody want
one?" A part of me died tonight.

*Mayweather vs. McGregor, August 26, 2017.

"Rodger Waters"

I'm glad Rodger Waters worked out his issues. Too bad he had to bring down three hundred million people with him.

"Eat Cake"

You're glamorous*
to me
and you don't even know it

I hang around famous people and they bore me

Happy Birthday
eat cake

*For Stephy Jo

"Tantra Hooker(Goals Part 2)"

My buddy, he tries to motivate me. He says I should make a list of everything I'd like to achieve for the day, so here goes:

1. Go through sound banks.
2. Fine tune script.
3. Call tantra hooker.

Time to practice piano.

"Wanna Date"

November 7, 2017

Hepatitis A: Negative.
Hepatitis B: Negative.
Hepatitis C: Wanna date?

"Hungry(Trains, Planes and USBs)"

I'm hungry right now,
I'll lie through my teeth
handin' off USBs
Implied NDAs

There's only one way to go into LA

Hungry.

"Motorbikes"

Blue collar guys talk. And talk and talk. I can tell it's
about work or somethin', I replace what they say
with stuff like "God I love her, I fucking love her."
The birds chirp, murmur, African-African-American
walks by with his kid, the noise is everywhere.
Motorbikes.

"22.(Can't be too Careful)"

22. I sat at table twenty-two. Went to the bathroom before the motherfuckers could seat me at twenty-eight again, not today homie,

22. Up against the wall, left-handed, only white dude in the place, what's new. Beef plate with the fish cake mindin' my own business, Asian lady's lookin' at me "I didn't do it."

22. She was older, balding, sixty-ish, "Here's some soup," she said. It looked good; cilantro, radishes, tiny pieces of carrot floating in a cloudy broth, it could be a trap. I grabbed the bowl and took a sip, I acted like I was choking. I stood up and pointed at her, I pointed right at her, "She did it, she did it!" Can't be too careful.

"So Lonely(My Shower)"

My, my shower's pretty big, I know I could fit two or three more people in here I'm so lonely.

"Binoculars"

Yeah, let's start the power-saw at 7:59 for five
minutes and silence. Two cups a coffee and I can't
clear my head, "Foreigner", I grew up on
"Foreigner".
Binoculars.

"Christian Rock"

If I were to write a "Christian Rock" song I'd call it "Amen".
Amen.

"Statues(Fakir Musafar/That is All Part 667.1)"

I wish they'd put up statues of Fakir Musafar. That is all.

"My Resume(Lynyrd Skynyrd '78)"

My resume:
1. I do dishes.
2. I give massages.
3. I have references.
4. DM me.

Lynyrd Skynyrd '78.

"Australia"

Sometimes when I'm dirty
I take a shower
And sometimes I let the water
run longer than I would if I were
in Australia
And I feel bad about it
but I let the water run
And run
the end.

"La Jolla Yoga"

I started yoga today, "La Jolla Yoga". Deep breath
ya'll.

"A Good Dentist"

A good dentist is everything.

"Coldplay"

I don't know much, but I do know one thing: "Coldplay" rocked San Diego last night, I'll never be the same.

P.S. Those guys are crazy.

P.P.S. Later.

"African Pepper(Land Race)"

When life gives you lemons, I smoke "African Pepper" land race sativa. Land race.

"James Cromwell"

Don't judge a book by its cover, James Cromwell is a "Black Panther".

"I'm Competitive Part 3(A Good Dentist Part 2)"

My dentist is better than your dentist.

"Man-Bun"

You've waited long enough, the man-bun is back.

"Fresno"

San Diego, 2017: A guy wearing a "You Are Beautiful" T-shirt. You don't get that in Fresno.

"The Easy Way"

The easiest way to get water out of your ears is to tilt your head sideways.

"Ben Stiller"

Ben Stiller is bi-polar. Ben Stiller is not from St. Louis.

"Black Sabbath"

My research shows that people that go to church get up earlier than people who listen to "Black Sabbath".

"Standing Rock"

I'm fasting for "Standing Rock" tomorrow. The meth should help.

"Frankie Goes to Hollywood"

"Frankie Goes to Hollywood" was not from was from St. Louis.

"Gaining Weight"

My friend, she tries to keep me down. Maybe I need it, maybe I don't. She says I've gotten stuck-up since I lost some weight. "I've been stuck up since I've been three years old," I tell her. "I'll gain the it back for ya, now that's love." She told me to have a good day, and to take care of myself. I'm pretty sure she hates me.

"Cat Leak"

I think it's pretty cool when my cat takes a leak at the same time as I do. It's kind of like when you queue up at the toilet with a good friend. I never queue up at the toilet with a good friend.

"Payday Loans"

Payday loans: Why we're better than Czechoslovakia. Take that Czechoslovakia.

"Clean Laundry"

I have clean laundry. Clean laundry is everything.

"Machine Gun Fun"

I had this great vision drivin' back from the dispensary, me and baby, I had on a leather vest and some 501's, she was wearin' some nipple clamps and the panties I like, and we were on this spinning platform and we both had machine guns, and we were shootin' motherfuckers for like twelve hours straight. When all the people were dead, I fucked her up the ass, we drove home, and watched a movie. The end.

"Bill Parcells"

Bill Parcells is an interesting guy but my favorite story is how he hired the same airline pilot to take his team back to the Super Bowl. That story just makes me shake my head(shakes his head).

"Van Halen"

What is Van Halen's favorite soup?

David Lee Broth

"Paper Clip(Here We Go Again)"

I had the paper clip in my pocket from the previous night you knew you'd need it the one-hitter was clogging but I choked down one more hit before I went to bed hash shatter Jack Herer were in there, I reached for it in the tiny pocket cops reach for and cleaned out my one-hitter here we go again.

"Interesting Fact #21"

"Sting" of "The Police" only jerks off once a year. That's probably the most disgusting thing I've ever written.

"Phone Plans(Part 2)"

The cool thing about paying sweetie's phone bill and not mine is now she can't call me to pay her phone bill.

"Next Year"

I was a better writer last year, sorry guys, maybe next year.

"Charlie Chaplin"

Charlie Chaplin was an Anarchist. I like Charlie Chaplin.

"My Friend"

My friend, nothin' bothers him. He does heroin, I think that helps.

"Locker Room Talk"

guru givin' me locker room talk now he's sittin' on the bench.

"Michael McDonald: Character Actor"

A lot of people ask me who's the most overlooked character actor in music videos. I always answer succinctly: "Michael McDonald".

"Leasing Agent"

A lady named "Lisa" sent me a text saying she was "interested in moving forward with the apartment". I replied "We've already rented it out, better luck next time". I'm not a leasing agent. I don't know any "Lisas". My life's perfect. The end.

"Sean Penn"

I met Sean Penn. The end.

"How I Cruise 'Backpage'"

How I cruise Backpage:

Search/Keyword/Prostate.

"Anarchy Guide Part 1"

Try heroin every day for two weeks and see if you like it. The end.

"Kurt Warner"

Kurt Warner: Great American. The end.

"Creative Writing Classes"

I will be offering creative writing classes(in my bed) this Spring. Hurry, classes are filling up fast.

"What Women Really Want Part 74"

What Women Really Want Part 74: Women are competitive.

"Turbulence"

There was some turbulence a few days back, my cat sleeps by my head.

"Laundry Part 2(Dry Cycle)"

I've re-written this "Laundry" piece ten times and it
still sucks, dry cycle man, do somethin' with the dry
cycle, I think I'm gonna do somethin' with the dry
cycle, I think you should do somethin' with the dry
cycle, I think I'm gonna do somethin' with the dry
cycle, I'm gonna do somethin' with the dry cycle. Dry
cycle. I think you should do somethin' with the dry
cycle, I'm gonna do somethin' with the dry cycle. Dry
cycle. Dry cycle. Dry cycle.
Dry cycle.

"What Women Really Want Part 76"

What Women Really Want Part 76: Women are practical.

"Andrew Cunanan"

I have a friend that partied with Andrew Cunanan.
The end.

"Support"

I would like to thank everyone who supported me through the name change, I really appreciate it. I'm having my penis cut off on Tuesday.

"Heroin Tap Part 4(That is All)"

Heroin tap, tap, tap. That is all.

"Twenty Years"

guy points
at counter lady
thats
are order married twenty years

"Jeff 'Skunk' Baxter"

I never knew I was going to grow up to look like Jeff "Skunk" Baxter. I'm not sure how I feel about that.

"Judge Judy"

Judge Judy's pissed. The end.

"Breaking News Part 22"

"Boneface" does not have what it takes to be "Ink Master".

"High Ridge, Missouri Part 3"

Tweaker with a laptop actin' all hard bring it.

"Dedication(Hard Drives/Cat Food Part 2)"

I'm only leaving the house to pick up cat food and hard drives. The end.

P.S. I need a prostate massage like you wouldn't believe.

P.P.S. Later.

"Creative Writing Classes Part 3(No Refunds)"

I still have two openings for the Spring semester of creative writing classes(in my bed). No refunds.

"Ween Girls"

spring leaves ween
ween girls in spring

"Steve Bartman "

Steve Bartman is a great American. Steve Bartman is not from St. Louis.

"Cranberry Sauce(Smoke Some Dope)"

Judy forgot the cranberry sauce again, she does this every year, can you send one of the boys up to get some cranberry sauce(smoke some dope).

"Molly"

There's a stop light right at the top of my hill it's a big one. I like to yell out "got any molly" when people get stuck at the light passes the time.

"Dear Fakebook(Part 3954%)"

Dear Fakebook,

I don't like Don Henley. The end.

"Dandelions"

who's they who What.
dandelion pick the Dressing.

"Is Stephie Jo Poly"

We've asked her. The message boards are goin' crazy. It's the talk of the whole underground "Ween" scene. "Is Stephie Jo Poly" on the next "Geraldo".

"Jackson Browne"

Jackson Browne smacked Daryl Hannah around. I forgive him.

"Meth is Good"

There's only one thing that's gonna get this country goin' again, and that's meth. "Meth: It worked under Clinton".

"Product Placement"

When you're so busy you pop open a "Coke" and you don't even have time to take a sip, that's dedication. That's product placement.

"Cat Leak Part 2"

I just took a leak with my cat.

"Roofies"

fresh batch of roofies

"Grammar"

From my brief experience on the "Facebook", I think people from the Midwest have incredible grammatical abilities. I'm from the Midwest.

"Deep Thoughts Part 1"

Thinkin' about gettin' a prostate massage.

"Furry"

Did a bunch of K, now I'm a furry

"A Real Solid(Good Fuckin' Chicken)"

I was diggin' sand, by hand, I thought I might be stuck, and I thought about the baby coyote I met the night before. You might think I'm crazy, but the moon was full, and he scared the shit out of me, I assume it was a boy, I'd just taken my contacts out, but like I said, the moon was bright, and my eyes ain't that bad. Anyway, back to the story. I'm stuck, diggin' sand, by hand, I'm not gonna die, but I am out there, Landers, California. I dug for awhile, and it didn't look good. I thought about walkin' for help. Fuck that. I got myself into this mess, and I'm gonna get myself out. I thought about the wood planks some good ol' boys put under my Eurovan a few years back. I collected rocks, a couple nice ones. I dug, by hand, I was actually having fun, it wasn't that hot of a day, and I had water. And weed. And pecan pie, what else does a man need? Anyway, I dug, and I dug, and it didn't look good. I dug, and I thought about the baby coyote I met the night before. Scared the shit out of me. And then, the baby coyote came to me, in a dream, or telepathic or somethin', and he was like, "Thanks for the chicken the other night," and I was like "You son of a bitch," I smiled. "That was good chicken, wasn't it?" I pause. "I got it from Walmart." The baby coyote smiled. I could tell he

212

wanted to give me a paw high-five or somethin' but we didn't have time for that shit. He gave me a look. "That was a real solid homie, a real solid". He gave me a nod, and took off. And I dug and I dug I and gave the hybrid another try; I'm out. I thought about the baby coyote. I thought about the lighter fluid I stashed behind a rock. I thought about the fire I started the night before. I thought about the baby coyote again. He gave me the nod. "That was good fuckin' chicken homie. Good fuckin' chicken." The end.

Tory Seller is an author, musician, filmmaker, screenwriter, comedian and performance artist. He divides his time between Denver and Los Angeles.